EVACUEES

OF THE

SECOND WORLD WAR

Mike Brown

SHIRE PUBLICATIONS

Published in Great Britain in 2010 by Shire Publications
Ltd, Midland House, West Way, Botley, Oxford OX2 0PH,
United Kingdom.
44-02 23rd Street, Suite 219, Long Island City, New York,
NY 11101, USA.

E-mail: shire@shirebooks.co.uk   www.shirebooks.co.uk

A CIP catalogue record for this book is available from the
British Library.

Shire Library no. 570 •   ISBN-13: 978 0 74780 745 2

Mike Brown has asserted his right under the Copyright,
Designs and Patents Act, 1988, to be identified as the
author of this book.

Designed by Ken Vail Graphic Design, Cambridge, UK
and typeset in Perpetua and Gill Sans.
Originated by PDQ Digital Media Solutions
Printed in China through Worldprint Ltd.

10 11 12 13 14   11 10 9 8 7 6 5 4 3 2

TITLE PAGE IMAGE
September 1939: a crowded evacuation train takes a girls'
school from the danger area. That many of the girls view it
as a great adventure can be seen on their faces.

CONTENTS PAGE IMAGE
The ideal of evacuation – happy children enjoying all the
glories of a country lifestyle. In reality this was not always
the case. (IWM D 2222)

ACKNOWLEDGEMENTS
I would like to thank The Kent Messenger Newspaper
Group for permission to use the front cover photograph,
and The Imperial War Museum (IWM), who have allowed
me to use illustrations, which are acknowledged at the
end of relevant captions accompanied by their reference
numbers. All other illustrations are from the author's
collection. I should also like to thank Pam Cleverly,
Maurice Cornelius, and David Wood, who kindly shared
their memories with me.

IMPERIAL WAR MUSEUM COLLECTIONS
Several of the photos in this book come from the Imperial
War Museum's huge collections, which cover all aspects
of conflict involving Britain and the Commonwealth since
the start of the twentieth century. These rich resources
are available online to search, browse and buy at
www.iwmcollections.org.uk. In addition to Collections
Online, you can visit the Visitor Rooms where you can
explore over 8 million photographs, thousands of hours of
moving images, the largest sound archive of its kind in the
world, thousands of diaries and letters written by people
in wartime, and a huge reference library. To make an
appointment, call (020) 7416 5320, or e-mail
mail@iwm.org.uk. Imperial War Museum
www.iwm.org.uk

CONTENTS

INTRODUCTION

A T THE END of August 1939, war was fast approaching. Many feared that it would be a war that would engulf Britain in a storm of fire, poison gas and high-explosive death, rained down by enemy aircraft on her towns and cities. With this fear in mind, the British Government gave the order that set in motion its evacuation scheme. Over two million civilians, most of them children, set off into the unknown, carrying a few meagre possessions, on what was to be the greatest shift in population since the industrial revolution a century before.

The Minister of Health at that time, Walter Elliott, described the evacuation as 'an exodus bigger than that of Moses. It is the movement of ten armies, each of which is as big as the whole Expeditionary Force.'

In towns and cities throughout Britain, the streets became full of groups of children, some carrying buckets and spades, who waved goodbye to tearful parents, as, school by school, they set off on long journeys by rail, bus, or even boat, into the countryside, on a scale never seen before or since.

This would prove to be just the first evacuation; a little over six months later, in the spring of 1940, with France falling, and Britain under the threat of imminent German invasion, the likely landing areas along the south-east coast saw a second round of evacuation. Then, as the Battle of Britain gave way to the Blitz, new waves of evacuees left, to be followed by yet more as the bombing targets changed and spread, and locations were evacuated, while the reception areas to which evacuees were sent shifted to the north and the west.

What had brought about this 'exodus', and how had such a massive enterprise been organized? How would the children, and others, fare in their new, and to many, alien enviroment? How did these city-dwellers cope settling into a new life in the countryside, and how did their new 'foster-parents' cope with their new, unexpected and sometimes unwanted families?

Looked at through official records, through advice, both official and unofficial, through newspapers, books and magazines of the time, and from the memories of those who experienced it, this book covers these and other questions to examine the many aspects of evacuation in the Second World War.

Opposite:
Young evacuees and nurse in the grounds of a country house. Many such country houses were used as evacuation hostels, especially for nursery schools. (IWM TR 247)

It might be YOU!

CARING FOR EVACUEES
IS A NATIONAL SERVICE

ISSUED BY THE MINISTRY OF HEALTH

BACKGROUND

DEATH FROM THE AIR first came to Britain on 19 January 1915, when a German Zeppelin dropped seven bombs over East Anglia, killing two people and injuring three. At the same time its sister ship bombed King's Lynn, accounting for two dead and thirty injured. On 31 May that year Zeppelin LZ 38 carried out the first air raid on London, causing seven deaths, four of them children, and thirty-five injuries.

There were, in all, fifty-three Zeppelin raids on Britain, mainly during 1915–16. These left 556 dead and 1,300 injured, the worst attack being on London on the night of 13/14 October 1915, which killed seventy-one. London was the main, but not the only target; Dover was heavily hit, and towns as widespread as Edinburgh and Portsmouth were attacked, with raiders concentrating on the Midlands, Norfolk, Suffolk and the Home Counties.

At first the Zeppelins were fairly safe from the defenders, as they could fly higher than the British fighter aircraft sent up after them, but advances in technology meant that this did not last long; new planes were able to fly higher and the 'Zeps' began to be shot down. However, similar advances meant the development of long-distance bomber aircraft to be used against Britain. From 1916 raids by groups of aeroplanes took place, sixty-three in all, mostly against the south-east. These caused 857 civilian deaths and 2,000 injuries, the worst raid being that of 13 June 1917, which led to 162 fatalities in Kent, Essex and London. By the time the final raid took place, on 19 May 1918, a total of 1,413 civilians had been killed, 670 of them in London.

Experience showed that it was impossible to stop a determined enemy from getting through; some might be shot down, but a blanket defence was impossible. Measures could be taken: air raid warnings would give people the chance to take cover; but where should this cover be? Ordinary houses and shops were increasingly vulnerable to direct hits as bombs got bigger; deep local features, such as the caves in Dover and elsewhere, the London Underground, or the basements of large buildings and the crypts

Opposite:
British government poster seeking helpers for the evacuation service.
HMSO

7

Above: Shelterers in the vaults of the Phoenix brewery in Dover in the First World War. Notice the prevalence of children.

Below: A contemporary postcard showing the after-effects of the Zeppelin raid on King's Lynn in 1915 which caused the first air raid deaths in Britain. There was a rather morbid fashion for such postcards at the time.

of churches offered sanctuary. Yet few of these places could be truly said to be bomb-proof to direct hits from the sort of very large bombs that the experts envisaged being developed in the future.

The public, however, had sought out such deep shelters in large numbers, that the government became concerned that, if one of these shelters were breached, the casualties would be horrendous and the blow against morale appalling. In 1917 a Cabinet Committee recommended a policy of 'dispersal' – encouraging the public to rely on the protection offered by their homes rather than to gather in crowds in a public place. Whilst there would be casualties, they would be spread over every raid, and in every place, rather than a huge number in one place at one time.

The end of the war in 1918 did not mean an end to planning. Any future European war would inevitably involve bombing, and, with continued aircraft development, this could be on a scale hitherto undreamed of.

THE RAIDER
PUBLICATION SANCTIONED BY OFFICIAL PRESS BUREAU.
PUBLISHING OFFICE: Copyright
39, ST. ANDREW'S HILL. E.C.

Above: Postcard from the First World War showing a zeppelin attack, searchlights and anti-aircraft explosions, almost certainly a mock-up.

Within three years of the end of the war the Air Raid Precautions (ARP) Committee of the British Home Office was set up to look at the problem of future air raids. It first met in May 1924; among the subjects discussed was the 'evoision', or, as we would call it, the evacuation, of civilians. This was an extension of the policy of dispersal; not just a move away from large communal shelters, but a parallel move away from crowded centres of population. This was not new; civilians had always had to pack up and move as war approached. During the First World War, many of those with the money to rent cottages, or who had relatives outside the cities, had sent their wives and children away from the danger areas.

The British government began to plan for widespread evacuation, carried out *before* a war began. Important industries, government departments and ordinary civilians not 'vital to the war effort' would be moved from the packed cities and spread across the country.

The ARP committee's early plans for evacuation, as it soon became known, were based on an onslaught on London, the heart of the nation, where both central government and also the War Office, Admiralty and Air Ministry were based.

Heavy German bomber, First World War. Bombers like these took over the air assault on Britain from the Zeppelins as the airships began to fall prey to British fighter aircraft.

One early idea was that in the lead-up to a future conflict, the entire population of the capital would be secretly evacuated at night, leaving London an empty city which could be bombed to rubble without loss of life, or disruption of government. This would be accomplished by the simple expedient of having the population head for the nearest railway or underground station and catch the first tube or train out of the centre, getting off at the end of the line. As a plan it sounds good, until it undergoes closer examination.

Apart from the logistical problems of transporting eight to ten million people with their pets and goods quickly, and, of course, in secret, out of the capital, no thought was given as to where they would go once they reached the outskirts, where they would sleep, who would feed them, and so on. Even ignoring this, the plan would inevitably cause absolute mayhem to government and vital industries as key workers and their families were scattered. This did in fact prove to be the case when in 1940, as the German army approached, the French government tried to evacuate itself from Paris to Tours; the ensuing disaster, with vital ministries out of touch with each other and the outside world, contributed to the country's collapse.

At the end of 1925 the ARP Committee published its first report, which established that it would be impossible to relocate much of the activity normally carried out in London, and that the nation could not continue to exist if bombing forced these activities to cease. The report split the population into two. The first group comprised those involved in vital war work, such as civil servants and workers in war industries, and others who were needed to support them – for example shopkeepers and servants. The second group consisted of those who played little or no part in the conduct of the war: women, children, the aged and the infirm. It was to this latter class that evacuation would apply.

The Committee understood that while it was desirable to evacuate this group from London, it would not be wise to try to do so compulsorily, as the accompanying element of force would only have a disastrous effect on morale. Instead the group must be convinced of the need to move, and encouraged and helped to do so. It was decided that the ministries of health and transport and the boards of education and trade should draw up schemes which would concentrate on the poorer areas; it was assumed that better-off families would make their own arrangements, as they had done during the First World War.

Work on these schemes moved at a snail's pace through the late twenties and early thirties, as the focus of attention shifted from a European war to internal problems: the economy, unemployment and the rise of socialism and communism. The enemy was now seen as the enemy within, the 'reds under the bed', rather than a foreign foe, an idea underlined by the General Strike of 1926.

Air-raid damage to a block of flats in Barcelona during the Spanish Civil War of the late 1930s. The British government sent experts to Spain to study the effects of bombing.

Above:
Poster issued by the Council for the Defence of Madrid. 'The Fascist airforce is flying over the capital of the Republic. What are you doing to take cover? Help Madrid'

Above right:
Poster: 'Evacuate Madrid' issued by the Council for the Defence of Madrid. Madrid suffered heavy raids during the Spanish Civil War.

Yet the plans were formed, however slowly. In 1931 the Warren Fisher committee reported to the government that, in a future war, Britain could expect 60,000 dead and 120,000 wounded on the *first day* of war alone, followed by 66,000 dead and 130,000 wounded per week thereafter. This stirred fresh interest in evacuation. By 1934, the focus of evacuation had changed: the size, speed, range and numbers of bombers meant that London was no longer regarded as *the* target. Towns, cities and industrial complexes throughout Britain were now in the firing line, and any evacuation scheme had to take this into account.

Over the next couple of years plans continued to develop in a rather sedate fashion with official advice still concentrating on individual rather than national schemes. The 1937 government booklet *The Householder's Handbook* suggested that, in an emergency 'If you live in a large town, children, invalids, elderly members of the household, and pets, should be sent to relatives or friends in the country, if this is possible.'

European events added another spur. The Spanish Civil War had broken out in July 1936 and air raids on the capital, Madrid, by the rebel Nationalist air force began at the end of August. In October support for the rebels arrived from Germany, including three squadrons each of Junkers Ju52 bombers and Heinkel He51 fighters. These aircraft of the Condor Legion,

as the German forces were called, had not only been sent to aid Hitler's ally, Franco; the war was a perfect training ground for German forces, and would prove invaluable in developing tactics, machines and aircrews for the war to come. Adolf Galland, later the chief of the Luftwaffe's fighter force, developed what became known as carpet bombing – using large numbers of aircraft to drop bombs on a single target in a short space of time, overwhelming both the target and the rescue and casualty services. Such a raid was carried out on the small town of Guernica in April 1937, where in just one afternoon 1,654 people were killed and 889 wounded.

The Republic's main towns and cities came under bombardment from the air, and evacuations took place. By the end of the war about 10,000 had been killed in the raids, dwarfing the 1,400 killed in Britain in the First World War, and underlining the huge death-toll expected in Britain in a future war.

In Britain, cinema newsreels showed the effects of the raids in Spain: collapsed and burning buildings, and rows of bodies covered in bloodied sheets. Even for those of limited imagination, the potential of air raids on other European cities was not lost, while European governments studied the raids in Spain, not, as the Germans did, for training their air forces, but to prepare their defences. As early as 1936 the French government set out an evacuation scheme under which everybody not vital to the war effort

Above left: Air-raid damage in Spain; a rescuer with a small child. Pictures such as this revived concerns about the effects of bombing in any future war, and gave fresh impetus to plans for evacuation.

Above: Poster: 'Evacuate Madrid'. During the Spanish Civil war many of the big cities were evacuated. The British government studied the situation there for use in a future war.

would be encouraged to leave the towns, whilst those who had to remain would be evacuated each night in a forerunner of what in Britain would become known as 'trekking' – leaving danger areas every night for the relative safety of the surrounding countryside.

By the beginning of 1938 British plans for evacuation were still theoretical. In May a 'Committee on Evacuation', comprising four MPs, was set up to look into evacuation, including other countries' schemes.

There would be different types of evacuation: first, as had taken place in the First World War, 'private' evacuation, where individuals made their own arrangements to leave the danger areas and seek accommodation either with friends and relatives or by renting. A second, new type of evacuation would be the official evacuation of those groups already identified: children, expectant mothers, the sick and the aged. The last thread would be 'business evacuation', whereby commercial and industrial concerns and non-vital government departments would move, as a unit, into less dangerous areas.

Of all these, the single largest group was the children, and this was the one that caused the most immediate concern to the general public. It was

Below:
Poster: 'What are you doing to stop this?' issued by the Spanish Republican Ministry of Propaganda.

Below right:
Poster issued by the Spanish Republican Ministry of Public Information; 'Homes. The finest hotels are converted into homes for refugee children.'

agreed early on that if the children were not with their families, then the best way to organise them would be by school.

This plan had many things in its favour: first, the children would be going with their friends, and in a voluntary system this would have the huge advantage of making them want to go, thereby increasing pressure on their parents to send them. Secondly the organisation involved would be immensely simplified; those operating the scheme (the teachers), would know the children and would be known by them and their parents. They were accustomed to dealing with groups of children on a daily basis and to giving instructions, and the children were, on the whole, used to obeying them. Lastly, relaying instructions and information to the parents was easily done, through notes home, or by the children themselves. Practice runs were equally easy to organise, and the marshalling area for the children – the school itself – was familiar.

As with any plan, the next phase became more problematic. It was the catch that had been glossed over in the earliest plans; where, once the evacuation had taken place, were the children to live? Even should the optimists be proved right and the war last just a few weeks, they would still need to be housed and fed for that time.

Below left: Poster issued by the CNT (National Confederation of Workers). In a chilling reflection of Hitler's words, the poster reads: 'Today Spain – Tomorrow the World'. The world seems to indicate France, to whom the Republic looked for aid, in vain.

Below: Poster issued by the Spanish Republican Ministry of Propaganda, with all the elements: hordes of aircraft and a dead child. Such images haunted many in Britain in the late 1930s.

Thank you, Foster=Parents . . . we want more like you!

Some kindly folk have been looking after children from the cities for over six months. Extra work? Yes, they've been a handful! . . . but the foster-parents know they have done the right thing.

And think of all the people who have cause to be thanking the foster-parents. First, the children themselves. They're out of a danger-zone — where desperate peril may come at any minute. And they're healthier and happier. Perhaps they don't say it but they certainly mean "Thank you".

Then their parents. Think what it means to them!

The Government are grateful to all the 20,000 people in Scotland who are so greatly helping the country by looking after evacuated children. But many new volunteers are needed—to share in the present task and to be ready for any crisis that may come. Won't you be one of them? All you need do is enrol your name with the local Authority. You will be doing a real service for the nation. You may be saving a child's life.

The Secretary of State, who has been entrusted by the Government with the conduct of evacuation, asks you urgently to join the Roll of those who are willing to receive children. Please apply to your local Council.

One of the ideas put to the Committee was to build 'camp schools' in rural areas. Housing about 500 pupils each, these would act as rural study centres in peacetime, with ten elementary schools taking turns to use the camp for a month each. In time of war, the camps would be expanded to hold all ten schools, and 5,000 pupils. Not only would the camps therefore serve both peace and wartime functions, but in the event of war both travel to the site and settling in there would be much aided by the schools' familiarity with the camp. The idea was warmly accepted, and further investigations were initiated, although it was accepted that the camps could only house a fraction of the evacuees.

The MPs reported back to the Home Secretary in July 1938, concluding that, in the main, housing evacuees could only be achieved in private houses using compulsory billeting powers, with the cost being borne, in the first place, by the government, although those able to do so should later be required to contribute towards their keep.

They further recommended that detailed plans for the evacuation of children of school age should be made on the school-by-school basis outlined above. Such a scheme, they believed, could be put together in just a few months. They correctly identified one of the main problems as how to encourage people to evacuate in a

Above: A rather tough-looking band of young evacuees, dutifully carrying their gas masks in a varied cross-section of cases, and displaying a good example of the types of everyday clothing worn by younger children at that time. (IWM D 824)

Postcard showing Prime Minister Neville Chamberlain, 'the pilgrim of peace', at the time of the Munich conference in 1938. Though it was widely lauded at the time, perceptions of the hand-over of the Sudetenland soon changed.

voluntary system, especially as this needed to be done before bombing started if widespread deaths were to be avoided.

The organisation at the school end was well under way, but that at the receiving end needed to be arranged, and the recently formed Women's Voluntary Service (WVS) was seen as the perfect vehicle for this. Within weeks its founder, Lady Reading, had made links with the Girl Guides and

British government
evacuation scheme
logo.
HMSO

Women's Institutes. Soon local Evacuation Committees were set up and County Evacuation Officers appointed.

In September 1938 it looked as if everyone's worst nightmare was coming true. Germany was demanding parts of Czechoslovakia on their joint border; the Czechs refused Germany's claim. Both countries prepared for war while Britain and France watched horrified; by treaty they would be drawn into conflict, just as they had been in 1914.

Defence measures were rushed forward; gas masks were issued to the public, trenches dug in parks, and a hastily put-together evacuation scheme for London schoolchildren emerged.

The WVS and Women's Institute was asked by the government to help local authorities in the reception areas carry out a house-to-house survey of possible accommodation, based on one person per habitable room. This identified almost five million possible billets, far more than would be needed.

The scheme for the evacuation of two million people from London, a quarter of them schoolchildren, was announced on September 29. Such was the air of panic that many had not waited; the railways reported passenger numbers of bank holiday proportions, mostly to Wales and the West Country. The Divisional Food Officer for South Wales reported that 130,000 people had arrived in his area in the first few days of the crisis. Under the government's plans, they were to be joined by 500,000 London schoolchildren on September 30, but the move was cancelled at the last minute as the Munich agreement, handing over the Sudetenland to Germany, was signed.

THE FIRST EVACUATION

THE EVACUATION SCHEME proposed before Neville Chamberlain briefly achieved peace at Munich was called off at the last minute. This came as a great relief, on the very day that half a million London schoolchildren were due to leave, but four thousand children from nursery and special schools had gone early; their experience demonstrated how close to disaster Britain thought itself.

Their move was accomplished with few problems, but on arrival most found themselves unexpected and unprepared for, with no billets organised, no food, and nothing else. In most cases the locals rallied round and barns or village halls became makeshift dormitories, while that British cure for everything, tea, was brewed and served by local housewives.

The children were safely back home again by 6 October, but no-one involved could pretend that the evacuation had gone smoothly; had it involved half a million children instead of four thousand, the result would have been mayhem. Even the government could not pretend otherwise; the Deputy Under Secretary of State at the Home Office could say no more than that the scheme would 'just about have stood up to the requirements of getting refugees out of London and bedding them down that night while we tried to sort out what was going to happen afterwards.'

The experience gained proved indispensable; the plan would form the bones of future evacuation schemes, but now it would be fleshed out. The focus shifted to ensuring that in any future evacuation arranging billets in advance would be a central part of the scheme. To do this the country was divided into three types of area: evacuation, reception and neutral. Evacuation areas were those likely to be bombed; in these areas 'priority' groups, that is children, pregnant women, the aged and the sick, would be given the opportunity to be evacuated at government expense in the event of a war. Reception areas were places unlikely to be targets, and would therefore receive evacuees, while neutral areas *might* receive raids, but in the short term they would not be evacuated; nor, however, would they receive evacuees.

Opposite:
Evacuees from Ealing arriving at the railway station carrying their few possessions in an assortment of bags, boxes and cases, under the watchful eye of a woman police constable.
(IWM HU 55937)

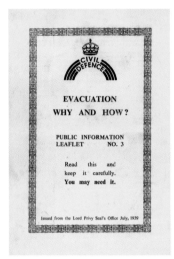

EVACUATION
WHY AND HOW?

PUBLIC INFORMATION
LEAFLET   NO. 3

Read   this   and
keep   it   carefully.
You may need it.

Issued from the Lord Privy Seal's Office July, 1939

Evacuation – why and how. This government leaflet setting out the evacuation scheme was delivered to every home in Britain in July 1939. HMSO

In July every house in the country received a leaflet entitled *Evacuation – why and how?*. This contained the following list of evacuation areas:

a) London, as well as the County Boroughs of West Ham and East Ham; the Boroughs of Walthamstow, Leyton, Ilford and Barking in Essex; the Boroughs of Tottenham, Hornsey, Willesden, Acton, and Edmonton in Middlesex

b) The Medway towns of Chatham, Gillingham and Rochester

c) Portsmouth, Gosport and Southampton

d) Birmingham and Smethwick

e) Liverpool, Bootle, Birkenhead and Wallasey

f) Manchester and Salford

g) Sheffield, Leeds, Bradford and Hull

h) Newcastle and Gateshead

i) Edinburgh, Rosyth, Glasgow, Clydebank and Dundee

In September the list was re-published, with the following proviso:

In some of these places only certain areas will be evacuated, as you have already been told. Evacuation may also be effected from a few other places, besides those above mentioned, of which you have been, or will immediately be, informed.

In January 1939 the government carried out a survey of the reception areas, which found that there was room for almost five million evacuees, well in excess of the three million expected. The Ministry then paired reception and evacuation areas; for example, the biggest evacuation area, Greater London, was to be evacuated to an area south of a line from the Bristol Channel to the Wash.

By the end of March all schools in evacuation areas were told how their school party would get to its reception area. Children from handicapped, special and nursery schools would be housed together in places such as stately homes.

In May, all those in the evacuation areas who qualified and wished to be included in the scheme had to register. Mothers of children under five could accompany their children, and take any older siblings with them, instead of sending them with their own schools. Conversely, in households where the children attended different schools, the younger children could all go with the eldest child's school, to keep the family together.

Throughout the summer rehearsals took place with children walking to their 'entraining stations'. Parents received lists of clothes, food etc., to have ready; these caused problems, as parents from poorer areas found that they did not have some items, such as pyjamas and wellington boots, and could not afford to buy them. A revised, shortened, list was published at the time of evacuation:

> Each child should have a handbag or case containing the child's gas mask, a change of under-clothing, night clothes, house shoes or plimsolls, spare stockings or socks, a toothbrush, a comb, towel, soap and face cloth, handkerchiefs; and, if possible, a warm coat or mackintosh. Each child should bring a packet of food for the day ... Mothers and other persons in charge of children below school age should take hand-luggage with the same equipment for themselves and their children as for school children... The names of the children should be written on a label or strong paper and sewn on to their clothes.

In the event many went carrying their possessions in a pillow case, which often included one toy – all they were allowed to take.

By August stocks of emergency food supplies for four million evacuees had been delivered to the receiving areas to ensure that evacuation would not cause a food shortage in the reception areas.

July brought the school summer holidays and a deteriorating international situation; Germany was demanding territory again, this time from Poland, and no-one was giving way. As war approached there were increasing calls for the government to begin evacuation before war broke

Evacuees from London's East End make their way to the railway station, accompanied by relatives. The children are wearing kit bags, many home made, and gas mask cases.
(IWM HU 36238)

Mothers and children at London's Victoria station, September 1939. The absence of tears is because these mothers were going with their children; mothers of younger children were given the option to do so. (IWM HU 36237)

out and the expected bombing started, but the government was loath to do anything that could be seen as preparation for war, and might thereby tip the balance, and so held back.

On 24 August the BBC broadcast a notice to teachers from evacuation areas to report back to their schools on the morning of the 26th, stressing that this did not mean that evacuation would actually take place. On Monday 28 August children in most evacuation areas were summoned to school, for a huge rehearsal. Three days later the Cabinet finally accepted the inevitable and the order to start evacuation on the following day was given.

The government tried to assure the public that this did not necessarily mean war:

> It has been decided to start evacuation of the schoolchildren and other priority classes as already arranged under the Government's scheme tomorrow, Friday, September 1. No one should conclude that this decision means that war is now regarded as inevitable.

The scheme swung into operation; notices were put up outside schools, notes were quickly sent, children's bags packed. On Friday morning the first school groups formed up in their playgrounds to walk in crocodiles to the local railway or underground station, or board buses or coaches, all to tearful farewells of the mothers and relatives who had accompanied them. Often the mothers walked behind or beside the crocodiles and relatives and friends came

Feeding young evacuees at a Women's Voluntary Service evacuation nursery. Such young children often adapted more quickly to evacuation than their older siblings. (IWM D 1692)

Evacuees from London's East End included children from the city's ethnic communities, such as this young boy. Sometimes they would encounter racism in the tight rural communities to which they were sent, where even people from the next village were looked on as 'foreigners'. (IWM S 5036)

out to wave goodbye. It was not unknown for children to be whisked away at the last minute by mothers who could not, when it came to it, face parting. Indeed, of the almost two million possible evacuees from London, only a third actually went, similar proportions going from the other evacuation areas. This meant that a very tight timetable was considerably eased.

Some children travelled by boat; pleasure steamers left boarding points along the Thames for east coast resorts. Buses were also used; some were on the road for up to two days. Green line coaches had been converted to ambulances carrying up to ten stretcher cases, to remove many of the capital's hospital patients in preparation for the expected air-raid casualties. But the majority travelled by train; in London special trains ran from the main terminals every nine minutes from 8.30 to 5.30 in a now finely honed plan. Every school knew which station it had to go to and how it was to get there, what train to get on, and where its final destination would be. Groups were synchronised to arrive at the stations so that the children would have less than fifteen minutes to wait. Midwives accompanied each party that included expectant mothers, and sighted guides accompanied blind evacuees.

It wasn't just London, of course; on the first day, 40,000 went from Leeds, while on the first two days

Above: Boarding an evacuation train, September 1939. Literally hundreds of such trains left the major cities over the first few days of September.

Right: Evacuees fixing on their labels. Most evacuees wore labels that identified which school group they belonged to, to help police or railway porters reunite them with their group if they became separated.

Left:
The common perception of evacuation is of children going by railway. This was not always the case; here a group of children are boarding a bus for their journey into the unknown.
(IWM D 2590)

Below:
Poster: 'Leave This To Us Sonny'. In spite of all the government's urging, there were still many children remaining in the cities when the Blitz began in September 1940.

37,000 were evacuated from Rochester, Chatham, Gillingham and Rainham, 30,000 from Southampton and Gosport and 22,000 from Birmingham; 36,000 went from Liverpool and Birkenhead and 6,000 from Middlesborough.

Robert Burns might have pointed to what happens to the best laid plans; this was a very tight timetable and the human factor played a large part. Some groups were late while others arrived very early, children became separated and at the stations themselves several groups would often arrive together, along with large numbers of servicemen returning to their units, to say nothing of the normal commuters and shoppers. The chaos that ensued can only be imagined; harassed stationmasters were faced with a train due to leave, but the school which was supposed to be on it had not turned up, whereas another school, not due for twenty minutes, had arrived, and were threatening to run riot. The temptation is obvious; the early school went in the other's place, and these 'best laid plans' began to unravel.

LEAVE THIS TO US SONNY — **YOU** OUGHT TO BE OUT OF LONDON

MINISTRY OF HEALTH EVACUATION SCHEME

Left: Cases, labels, and tears. Evacuation from Chatham, site of a naval dockyard on the river Medway in Kent. (IWM HU 59253)

Below: Evacuees being given drinks at the railway station. Long train journeys, sometimes in trains without toilets, would be made less uncomfortable by such kindness. (IWM HU 65886)

Girl Guides taking care of evacuee babies. Like the WVS, the Guides did a great deal of useful work with evacuees.

Many of the special trains needed for the evacuation were put together from old rolling stock kept moth-balled for emergencies. Many of them were non-corridor compartments, and, as can be seen from contemporary photographs, the children were often packed into them, with three or four squeezed into seats designed for two.

The children had been told to bring a packed lunch with them but, as with any school journey, many of these were eaten as soon as the children got on the train. Often the trains made frequent stops, and at each one the WVS or the Girl Guides or others were there, distributing drinks, biscuits or sandwiches; one evacuee remembered, 'A lady in a green uniform [WVS] and large hat, leaned in the window and gave us all a little packet of nuts and raisins and an orange.' All these drinks began to have their effect, and the combination of this and the lack of corridors caused another problem, for which the windows gave a ready solution. David Wood recalled, 'there was no corridor and I can vividly remember the boys peeing out of the window'. In some places the authorities had thought of this; children passing through Petts Wood in Kent were taken off the train to a field where ditches had been dug over which were placed planks, in pairs, with a gap in between, making crude, but effective toilets. Sadly these planks were somewhat roughly finished, and, as one evacuee remembered, splinters meant a painful continuation of the journey.

The trains were often slow; many evacuees speak of being repeatedly shunted on to sidings while express trains passed, or of taking meandering routes. Thus journeys which would normally take an hour or so became five-or six-hour marathons. Combined with the cramped conditions, the early packed lunch and the snacks, it was not surprising that on arrival at their destination they would be met with horror at their dishevelled and dirty appearance. Not only that; the original plan had called for the children to be medically examined before the evacuation, but as it happened during the holidays this did not take place. The cramped move thus meant that if one child in a compartment had head lice then every child in the compartment got head lice, and likewise any other communicable disease.

On arrival at their destination – not, as we have seen, always the destination they were expecting – they were often met by local organisations, including children's groups such as Guides or Scouts. Maurice Cornelius was a Wolf Cub with the 1st Dawlish pack:

Scouts helping evacuees, November 1940. Many voluntary groups such as the Scouts helped with the movement and reception of evacuees.

> The Cub Master and his assistant gathered some of us cubs together in order to meet and greet the evacuees, we were handed games and toys to try to make the new arrivals feel comfortable and wanted. We walked from the railway station to a building known locally as The Hut.

Left: After an often long journey, a meal was the first necessity on arrival for evacuees, still sporting their labels.

Next they had to be found billets: enter the local billeting officer. These would have lists of locals who had been found in the January survey to have space for evacuees. Sometimes the evacuees arrived so late that they had to sleep in the church hall that night; earlier arrivals often faced what many called the 'cattle market'. Locals had no choice but to take evacuees if they had the space, but were somewhat mollified by being allowed to choose their 'vacees'. Thus children were herded into a hall where the local people came and chose them, rather like picking sides in a children's game. Sometimes the children were even told to march round the room in pairs so that people could get a better look.

Those remaining at the end of the day were taken by the billeting officer to houses that had not taken their evacuees, to be presented at the door of many an unwilling and disgruntled 'foster-parent', as billeters were officially known. On arrival, children were given special postcards on which to fill in their address to let their parents know where they were.

This first part of the evacuation process was generally considered a huge success, and the

Below: Billeting officer, left, helping a billeter to fill in a form, probably a claim for shoes or clothing, for her two evacuees. Clothing growing evacuees was often a real problem for billeters. (IWM D 5081)

Right: Address card. These were given to evacuees to fill in their new addresses so that parents would know where they were as soon as possible, and also that the children had arrived safely.

Below: Billeting officer delivering evacuees to their new home; the children of the family look genuinely quizzical at the new arrival. Would they get on together?

FROM

Daphne Clapham

c/o South Park School I 34

35, Gainsborough Road,

Ipswich,

Suffolk.

Write in **BLOCK** letters and if possible in ink. Be sure to show correct postal address.

This is my new address. Please address letters correctly as shown above.

P. 486B.   51–3583

[TURN OVER

government reported it to have gone without a hitch. This was a rather rosy picture of the event, designed to reassure parents naturally concerned about their children. But all in all, considering the scale of the event, and its uniqueness, it could have been far worse, and was indeed infinitely better than would have been the case eleven months earlier, at the time of Munich. Most of the hitches were fairly minor and were soon ironed out.

Back in the towns and cities there were a few problems, too; the RSPCA in London reported hundreds of school pets left behind; they had to deal with dogs, cats, rabbits, guinea-pigs and birds, 'to say nothing of three young alligators that one school had decided to adopt.'

The 'Second Great Trek' as this first wave of evacuation was called, was completed. There now followed the even greater task of settling nearly 1.5 million official evacuees into new homes, schools and families.

One of the problems of evacuated schools was to find suitable buildings for teaching. Here two different classes are being taught in a village hall in Carmarthen. (IWM D 1052)

EVACUEE LIFE

After an often frenzied and chaotic move came the task of settling in to billets. This was in many cases to prove traumatic; many of the evacuees had never been parted from their families before; most of the poorer children had never even left the area they lived in. For most, the regional accents and food would prove strange and, at first, forbidding, and their welcome from often unwilling billeters in many cases left much to be desired.

Whereas evacuation was voluntary, taking evacuees was not, and depended on the space in your house, and the billeting officer. Some who were quite happy to take the odd evacuee found themselves with much more on their hands; Pam Cleverly remembers that, 'The population of our three bedroom semi had doubled on September 1st, when my mother was persuaded by the billeting officer to take Mrs Smith, her daughter Norma, aged nine, and Mavis Franklin, aged ten, instead of the one girl she had requested.'

The *Daily Telegraph Guide to ARP* had tried to reassure the public:

> This is not to suggest that compulsion would be necessary; but it is certain that mere unwillingness to accommodate a child, mother or teacher would not be accepted as a valid excuse unless there were good domestic reasons to justify it. Householders, it may be noted, would not be expected to take in expectant mothers, unless it were understood that confinement would be in maternity homes or, in difficult cases, in hospital. Large empty houses would be temporarily converted into maternity homes, and an adequate supply of midwives is now being recruited. Large houses are also being earmarked for mentally and physically handicapped children and for unaccompanied infants. Many owners of big country houses have been generous enough to turn over their property unconditionally for this purpose.

The pill was sweetened; everyone taking in unaccompanied schoolchildren received 10s. 6d a week in advance if one child was taken, and 8s. 6d a week each for more than one. This was to cover board, lodging and 'all the care necessary to give the child a home'. It was *not* for medical expenses, which

Opposite:
A typical publicity shot of the period – young evacuees exploring their new rural surroundings.
(IWM D 3106)

'My little evacuee' postcard – the card says it all.

A billeting officer's card. The billeting officer was in charge of placing evacuees in suitable lodgings or 'billets', and for sorting out any subsequent problems that might arise.

were to be paid by the local authority, or clothes, for which the child's parents were responsible.

For children accompanied by their mother, or other adult, the householder received 5s. a week for each adult and 3s. a week for each child. The government assured billeters that:

> These payments would cover shelter and access to water and sanitary accommodation. You would be under no obligation to give any other services, but the Government feel sure you would wish to do all you could to help the children and their mothers forced suddenly to leave their homes and families and finding themselves in strange surroundings. It would be particularly appreciated if you could make cooking facilities available.

On first arriving the evacuees were issued with emergency food supplies for forty-eight hours, which were given to their billeter. These usually consisted of canned meat or fish, milk, biscuits and chocolate. After this time the stockpiled food reserves would have been issued to the local shops.

Young evacuees enjoying an art lesson at their evacuation hostel, Dartington Hall. (IWM D 30703)

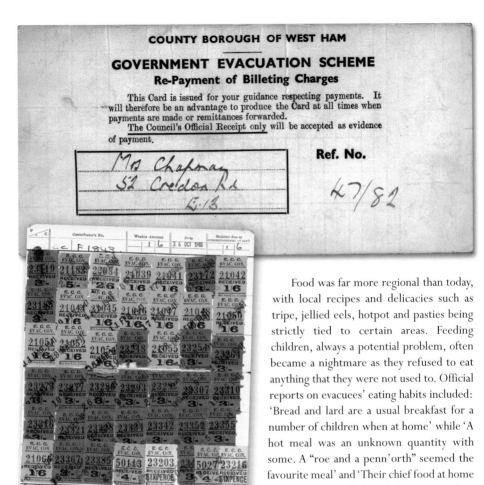

After the dust had settled, those who could afford it were asked to pay towards the cost of their children's keep. These two contribution cards are from West Ham, and Ilford in Essex.

Food was far more regional than today, with local recipes and delicacies such as tripe, jellied eels, hotpot and pasties being strictly tied to certain areas. Feeding children, always a potential problem, often became a nightmare as they refused to eat anything that they were not used to. Official reports on evacuees' eating habits included: 'Bread and lard are a usual breakfast for a number of children when at home' while 'A hot meal was an unknown quantity with some. A "roe and a penn'orth" seemed the favourite meal' and 'Their chief food at home was in most cases fish and chips, more often the latter without the fish. Milk puddings were unheard of and some did not even know what a pudding was.' Even more alarming, 'Few children would eat food that demanded the use of teeth – in almost every case could only eat with a teaspoon,' and 'Practically all disliked fresh vegetables and pies and puddings of fresh fruit, plums, damsons, etc., were quite unknown to them.' The report goes on in a manner reminiscent of Jamie Oliver:

One little girl of 5¹/₂ remarked one day that she would like to have beer and cheese for supper... Most of the children seemed under-nourished when they arrived, yet some were troublesome to feed, not liking stewed fruit, vegetables and jam. Children had been used to receiving a penny at home to buy their own dinners. One used to buy broken biscuits, the other Oxo cubes... Most of them seemed quite unaccustomed to ordinary everyday food and preferred a 'piece' or a bag of chips on the doorstep... Those from the most neglected homes had no idea of eating at table, but were expert in making anything into a sandwich, fingers being preferred to forks... Soup seemed to be unknown to some of the children. One mother admitted they never had soup, while two boys (10 and 12) attempted it with a knife and fork.

What is even more shocking is the widespread nature of these reports, covering, as they do, children from London, Leeds, West Bromwich, Manchester, Liverpool and Newcastle.

It had been planned that all children would be medically inspected before evacuation, but this had not taken place; in many cases local doctors and nurses carried out the examination at the receiving end, and the 'nit nurse', whose job it was to deal with cases of head lice, was often kept hard at work for the first few weeks. Children with communicable illnesses were usually put into special hostels, often large country houses either loaned to the government by their owners or in some cases requisitioned for the purpose.

Another unpleasant side to evacuation was bed-wetting, often caused by the shock of children being taken from their families. Some months after the

An evacuee feeding centre in a village hall. Such centres were often set up to accommodate evacuee children after school. Here they are having 'tea', seemingly oblivious to the preparations for the local amateur dramatic production.
(IWM D 5658)

Above: Evacuees looking a little apprehensively at beehives. Education for the evacuees often included such rural crafts as beekeeping. (IWM D 813)

EVACUATED SCHOOLS at WARMDENE, PATCHAM.

··◻◻◻···

SPORTS DAY, 1940.

··◻◻◻···

This is to certify that *Eileen Cox* of *St Mary's* School was successful in gaining *1st* Place in the *Fun race*.

S. E. Hodder A.T.C.L. L.G.S.M.
Head Teacher.

Date *July 2nd 1940*

Right: Sports certificate for evacuated school children July 1940.

original move hostel places were made available for incurable bed-wetters, and from mid 1940 an allowance of around 3s 6d a week was payable to householders with enuretic evacuees. Hostels also began to take in 'problem' and disturbed evacuees, much to the relief of their much-put-upon billeters.

Disciplining evacuees became a much-debated subject. It often added to an already fragile relationship between billeters, or foster-parents as the government preferred them to be called, and natural parents, over things like paying for children's clothes. It opened the whole Pandora's box of what was 'appropriate' behaviour from the children, and what was the appropriate response to rule breaking. As late as December 1940, the *Sunday Dispatch* was reporting that 'The courts are soon to decide whether a foster-parent of an evacuated child has authority to chastise for misbehaviour. The right to punish "reasonably" is given to a schoolmaster, but foster-parents do not yet know what their rights are.' Some evacuees went even further; there was a great deal of grumbling about pilfering from local shops and petty vandalism. As is often the case, locals were quick to point the finger of blame at the 'vaccees' as they became called, not always without cause. Some evacuated children finished up before the magistrates, where they were on occasions threatened with compulsory return to their old homes, but borstal or an evacuation hostel was the usual outcome.

Schooling was another challenge; where only one or two children were new to an area, they could easily be absorbed into the existing school, but where, as was often the case, an entire school had arrived, a creative solution was required. This was usually achieved by sharing the local school; the local children and teachers using the building in the morning, and the 'incomers' in the afternoon, or vice versa. This was the system set up by several public and grammar schools that had arranged their own form of private evacuation by 'twinning' with a similar school in an evacuation area, thus ensuring the use of suitable premises.

Maurice Cornelius, a local schoolboy from Dawlish, South Devon, remembers:

> What was good as far as the local children were concerned, was that because the schools were not big enough or equipped to take extra numbers, and as it was necessary for the evacuees to mix as quickly as conveniently possible with their own age group, the class numbers were very large. The decision was made locally to reduce the number of classes attending school at any one time. So this meant we were occupied elsewhere in

Song sheet
Evacuees in Wales –
including the line
''til the peril's past
and we're safe at
last we'll be safe in
the land of Wales'.

"Evacuees in Wales"

Dedicated to
J. EDWARD MASON, M.A., M.Ed.,
DIRECTOR OF EDUCATION, CARMARTHEN

Price 3d.

Copyright by
R. G. FREYNE, 62 Norfolk Crescent,
SIDCUP, KENT

Printed in Great Britain

After the rush to evacuate the children in September 1939 was over came the problem of finding suitable 'schools'. In the meantime many classes took place outside.
(IWM HU 36236)

'picking potatoes' for local farmers, creating gardens at our school, looking after pigs in the school piggery etc.

At the local schools, the evacuees would receive a hot meal in the middle of the day, a new thing for many. Schools would also arrange after-school amusements, games and exercises to keep the younger children amused until dinnertime, while older boys were encouraged to work on the land.

This was, of course, the biggest change for many evacuees, the move from an urban to a rural environment, which often seemed at first strange and hostile. Everything was different, the sights, the sounds, including the

Lack of suitable teaching accommodation could, in good weather, be made up for by al fresco classes, as here in Carmarthen.
(IWM D 1048)

Left: Evacuated
children from
Deptford enjoying
the country life in
Pembrokeshire
in a scene repeated
throughout Britain's
country areas.
(IWM D 974)

Below right:
Ploughing – older
boys such as these
were welcomed
in farming areas,
where they could
be a real help
around the farm
at a time when
domestic food-
production was vital
to Britain's survival.
(IWM D 2473)

local accents, the smells – especially the smells – and even the silence at night. But many of the children soon learned to appreciate their new surroundings. The press published photographs of evacuees enjoying their new rural life, reassuring worried parents that their children were having a wonderful time. Amusing stories were published of evacuees' amazement that milk did not originate in bottles, and the fact that some did not know what a cow or sheep was.

Below: Sillince
cartoon: spring.
Evacuated town
children's delight
at the joys of the
countryside was
a continual source
of humour.

For some the reality was more harsh as they faced growing accustomed to living without electricity, gas or running water, and long hours working on the land, sometimes maltreated, often resented by their unwilling foster-families and by the local community.

Norah Bearing writes of just such local resentment in *A Friendly Hearth*. She had set up a small evacuee hostel in Wales:

> Next came the barber. I sent all the little boys with sixpence each – the price given on the list in his window – to have their hair trimmed. They returned crestfallen and still shaggy. The price for the Welsh was indeed sixpence – for evacuees ninepence. Off I went to interview the gentleman in his tiny shop. Why, I asked, were my children asked to pay more than the stipulated price? He withstood all my raving at this injustice and attempted robbery. He had enough customers – besides it was a risk he would be taking to cut the hair of these little English – they are so dirty. If I cared to pay him a certain sum each month he would come and cut the hair at the house; it would be after his working hours, of course, and he would expect to make a little extra.

The weather in September 1939 was glorious – here evacuees in Buckinghamshire are enjoying the fine weather, and carrying their gas masks; soon few gas masks would be carried even when not swimming! (IWM HU 36213)

It was little wonder that with such difficulties, and the non-appearance of the expected mass-bombing, a steady trickle of evacuees started to return home, a trickle that threatened to become a flood. Pam Cleverly recalls, 'The evacuees were not with us for very long. Several got together and rented houses in the town and because nothing happened they had all returned home before Christmas 1939.'

Mothers who had evacuated with their children were especially prone to return, either worried or suspicious about their husband's new-found bachelor life.

"THINKIN' OH! MY DARLING LOVE OF THEE!"
(WITH APOLOGIES TO CYRIL FLETCHER.)

Above: 'Thinking oh my darling love of thee'; a hard-pressed husband forced to take care of himself reflects on his wife and daughter in their new evacuation home.

Below: Sheet music *Goodnight Children Everywhere* by Joe Loss's orchestra. Note the dedication.

The government worked hard to persuade evacuees to stay; 'Leave the Children Where They Are', the posters read. As early as 13 September 1939, the *Daily Mirror* reported 'Plans for Reshuffle of Evacuated Families':

To 'relax tension' caused by having two families in one house under the evacuation scheme, the Minister of Health, Mr. Walter Elliot, suggested that there should be communal meals for mothers and young children including schoolchildren.

'Some of the people evacuated from Birmingham slums have gone back to their homes because, they say, their billets were too 'posh'. Others have returned home because they were billeted in a miner's cottage. They complained that

they had to go out for a stroll while the miner took his bath.'

The article went on to warn that:

In cases where people wish to return home, local authorities are asked to warn them that the evacuation scheme was planned for the children's safety; that if they return they will be taking a serious responsibility on themselves; and that evacuation facilities will not be provided if they change their minds again.

In spite of this, of the nearly 1.5 million official evacuees, more than half had returned home by Christmas.

Above: A Ministry of Health poster urging mothers not to bring their children back from evacuation during the 'Phoney War' period. In spite of this many did return as the expected bombing did not materialise. HMSO

Right: A Sillince cartoon: the Christmas party. Country houses often played host to large parties of young evacuees, and at Christmas grand parties often took place, to the enjoyment of everyone, except, perhaps, the old gentleman on the right.

Opposite: Evacuees' Christmas party in an evacuation hostel. Christmas was a particularly bad time to be away from one's family, and evacuees were often treated to Christmas parties; much to the resentment of the local children. (IWM D 5704)

OTHER EVACUATION

BUSINESS EVACUATION

WHEN WE THINK of evacuation we picture children with labels, but they were not the only evacuees. There was business evacuation where whole offices or factories moved out of the danger areas, often to large country houses rented for the purpose, with workers housed in hostels, or billeted in the local area.

This evacuation was to the 'neutral' areas, which the *Daily Telegraph* reminded its readers were:

> not suitable as reception areas for children, but they usually fringe the big cities, and would be useful for the business community. They certainly offer more security than such places as the City of London. It is understood that for certain essential businesses – and probably a big proportion of Whitehall – arrangements are being made to billet the staffs with householders in the neutral areas.

One such business was the BBC, vital for Britain's morale, and for passing on official information to the public. Before war was declared elaborate plans were made for the dispersal of the various departments to safer areas, so that broadcasting could be kept going. In his book *ITMA*, Francis Worsley, a BBC producer, described what happened:

> John Watt, the Director of Variety, told me to go home and await instructions. I lived in the country and was fairly cut off, and what with one thing and another I never heard what the vital signal was to be. Actually it was a word cue on the air. When the announcers started to say 'This is London' instead of 'This is the National Programme' we were to start. I consequently remained in the country trying frantically to get London on the phone.

Between 3 and 6 September 1939, production moved to three separate centres 'somewhere in England'. A 'Variety Centre' was set up in Bristol; the religious

Opposite:
For a short period in the summer of 1940 evacuee children were taken by ship to such places as the USA, by the Children's Overseas Reception Board, CORB (notice the armband, lower left). This group is embarking for Australia.
(IWM HU 36216)

Right: Young evacuees enjoying the countryside. For many inner-city children this was their first experience of life outside the city. (IWM TR 248)

Below: Business evacuation. Staff of the Atlas insurance company moving home from the City of London to Kingswood in Surrey, 26 August 1939.

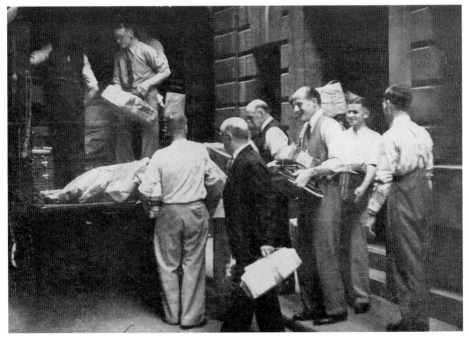

department went to Bedford, while in Evesham a large mansion, Wood Norton, was converted into offices and emergency studios where the drama department was installed. Meanwhile the locals had to get used to the appearance in their area of 'bohemian' types sporting beards and eccentric outfits.

Parallel to business evacuation was evacuation of government, where whole departments were moved from London, such as the Ministry of Food, which was transferred to Colwyn Bay in Wales, or the Admiralty, which went to Bath. Billeters were paid twice as much for these civil servants as for children, 21 shillings, one guinea, a week, from which came their less than flattering nickname 'Guinea Pigs'.

Ww O 4752

ASSISTED TRAVEL TICKET
— FOR —
EVACUATED WAR WORKERS

IN	DATE VALID FROM	OUT
X Trans		Trans. X
Mon day	AVAILABLE BETWEEN	Mon day
Tues day	AND	Tues day
Wedn sd'y		Wedn sd'y
Thur sd'y	SIX (6) SEVEN (7) : **DAYS** TRAVEL BY	Thur sd'y
Fri day	1.	Fri day
Satu rd'y	2. 3. 4.	Satu rd'y
Sun day	S. D.	Sun day
MALE	**Fare** :	FEMALE

FOR CONDITIONS OF ISSUE SEE BACK.
Bell Punch Company Limited, London. 8-41

Above: Business billet: Eyhurst Court, the new home of the evacuated Atlas insurance company. Many such evacuated businesses leased country manors such as this. The building on the right is the staff canteen.

Left: Assisted travel ticket for an evacuated war worker. Business evacuees were often billeted some way from their company's temporary place of work, and these subsidised tickets went some way to make up for this.

51

PRIVATE EVACUATION

For those who did not qualify for the official scheme, there was 'private' evacuation. The *Daily Telegraph* in August 1939 informed its readers that:

> You are entitled to make arrangements with friends or relations in the country for the reception of your wife, children or other suitable members of the family. It would be unwise to rely upon there being any rail transport available for such private movements in the first four days of emergency. Motoring might also be drastically restricted, with a view to keeping the main roads clear and to conserve fuel supply. Private movement must be made, therefore, before or after the official evacuation takes place, preferably before even at the risk of a wasted journey.

In its *War Emergency Instructions and Information* of September 1939, the government advised:

> Persons who make their own arrangements to move from one part of the country to another should take food sufficient for one or two days with them. This is to prevent a sudden new demand being made upon local shops before steps can be taken through ordinary channels to increase their supplies.

A happy-looking group of evacuees in Totnes. The pain of leaving their families was often made more bearable by being amongst a large group of school friends.
(IWM D 2243)

In his book *Problems of Social Policy*, R. M. Titmuss estimated that between June and September 1939, two million people were privately evacuated.

About this time adverts appeared in newspapers and magazines for hotels in 'quiet areas', 'safe areas', or just 'evacuation areas'. Another option, for those who could afford it, was to rent a house in the reception areas. As the war went on and previously safe areas came under threat, many who had rented such houses moved to new safe areas, sometimes moving several times as the air assault changed targets. This became known as 'bomb-dodging'. Norman Longmate, in *How We Lived Then*, records that:

> To have seven or eight homes, none of them permanent, during these six years was not at all uncommon, and altogether during this period sixty million changes of addresses were recorded in England and Wales in a population of thirty-eight million.

Some went further, literally; in the lead-up to the war some began to go overseas:

> furriers, costumiers, jewellers, modistes and antiquarians started exporting their commodities as fast as possible, following them with their wives, their showgirls and, finally, themselves. The amount of invisible exports which left the country in the first year of the war will never be known.
> (Maurice Edelman, *Production for Victory, Not Profit!* 1941)

For those without the money or contacts, the alternative was 'trekking', where people from heavily-blitzed towns would leave each evening to avoid the raids, camping out in the surrounding countryside, or sleeping in the backs of vans, to return next morning.

CONTINUING EVACUATION OF SCHOOLCHILDREN
Small-scale evacuation continued throughout the winter of 1939/40; a second wave of two-thirds of a million children was planned in February. This time parents had to sign an undertaking that they would definitely send their children and that they would leave them in the reception areas until the school party returned. It met with a poor response, which was, perhaps, just as well; more than half of those children who did try to join their evacuated schools found that they had to wait months while billets were found.

SCHOOL CAMPS
The 1939 Camps Act proposed fifty countryside camps, each to act as a complete evacuation school. In the event only thirty-one were constructed; the first being completed early in 1940; by mid-1941, thirty were in use,

One of the thirty-one school camps set up by the government. These were, in effect, self-contained schools set up in the countryside with dormitories, dining room, hospital and lavatory block, housing about 200 older pupils each. HMSO

housing over 6,000 children. Each was fully contained, with classrooms, dormitories, dining room, hospital and lavatory block, all made of cedar. As well as the usual subjects, pupils were taught gardening, pig and poultry keeping, shoe repair and house management. They cost around 25 shillings a week per pupil, but parents were only charged the normal billeting fees, the government footing the remainder.

From March 1940 unaccompanied children under five became a priority. Those nurseries that had been evacuated had nowhere near enough space to fulfil the demand, so new ones were set up by voluntary bodies or by local authorities. Within a year 6,000 children had been accommodated, rising to 13,000 by the end of 1942.

THE SECOND EVACUATION

Spring 1940 brought the German *Blitzkrieg* on western Europe, culminating in the fall of France. Britain was next; a German invasion of the east or south-east coast was expected at any time, and the evacuation of these areas, widely used as reception areas in 1939, began on 19 May with the removal of 8,000 children who had been evacuated to Kent, Essex and Suffolk.

Plans were hastily prepared; children previously evacuated to areas south of a line between the Wash and Newhaven were moved farther afield, joined by children living in the threatened areas, and from inland towns likely to be bombed. The new reception areas were Berkshire, Somerset, Devon, Cornwall and Wales. As these entailed a long railway journey, the Ministry of Health asked the railways to provide hot meals and drinks, to which they agreed, and from November hot meals were served at a shilling each, while milk was provided on shorter journeys.

Take-up of the first evacuation had not been overwhelming, and of those who had gone, many had already returned. To encourage children to take part in this second evacuation, schools in London, still regarded as the main target, were closed for a week, and by the middle of June over 100,000 children had been moved. Lessons learned in September were applied: every child was medically inspected before leaving and all evacuees had to take with them a minimum of clothing; any not having enough would have any shortages made up.

Another lesson learned was that many children had been snatched back at the last minute by mothers who had gone with them on a tearful trek to the station; this time the parents were asked not to go to the stations, and those who did were usually refused access to the platforms.

With the summer of 1940 came the threat of invasion. The south and east coast towns of England, possible invasion sites, were evacuated, and children, such as these boys from Lowestoft, were moved to the west.
(IWM HU 52715)

Right: Mothers at London's Waterloo station. In the first evacuation relatives were allowed to say goodbye at the train, but several children were snatched back at the last minute by parents who could not face parting. In later evacuations, like this one, parents were stopped at the platform gates.

Below: Evacuees to the West Country enjoying life in the tents of a temporary camp. (IWM HU 7089)

Below right: Wales and the West Country became the main destinations for evacuees from the South and Midlands after the invasion scares of 1940. Here evacuees are being taught to speak Welsh. (IWM HU 36235)

This evacuation, taking place as it did over several weeks, was known as 'trickle' evacuation. Between July and August, nearly a quarter of a million children, half from London, were evacuated, though once again the take-up was disappointing.

The problem of finding appropriate billets remained; in June the government agreed to supply free travel vouchers and to pay a billeting allowance to mothers of children under school age from evacuation areas, if they arranged their own accommodation. This 'assisted private evacuation scheme', as it was called, met with some success, and from October it was extended to include all evacuable adults in the Greater London evacuation area, and in December to unaccompanied children, while the scope of the scheme was widened to include transfer to Northern Ireland and Eire.

MH.

CHILDREN'S OVERSEAS RECEPTION BOARD.

45, BERKELEY STREET,
W.1.

C.O.R.B. Reference:

S/577

Your Reference:

Telegrams:
Avoncorb, London.

Telephone:
MAYFAIR 8400

2nd October, 1940.

Dear Madam,

    I have been directed to express to you the gratitude of this Board for the splendid way in which you came forward to help, and for the way in which you carried out your often arduous duties on board ship. It must be gratifying to you that you won the affection of the children and the respect and admiration of those who served with you.

        Yours truly,

        G. McNeill-Moss

        (Dgn)

Miss.I.Westerman,
39,Porchester Square,
London, W.2.,

OVERSEAS EVACUATION

After the fall of France, the British government received offers from Commonwealth countries and the United States to take evacuee children. An Overseas Evacuation Scheme was set up, run by the Children's Overseas Reception Board (CORB), which provided free passage for children to the USA, Newfoundland and Canada. CORB received 200,000 applications by early July, and by August the first 'seavacuees', as these children became known, sailed for America.

The scheme was short-lived; on 30 August, the SS *Volendam*, carrying seavacuees, was torpedoed, but luckily all passengers were rescued. Two weeks later, however, on 17 September, the SS *City of Benares* was sunk with the loss of seventy-three seavacuees, and further government overseas evacuation was cancelled; by this time 2,700 children had already gone to America, where they remained until the end of the war.

CHANNEL ISLANDS

On 16 June 1940, with France falling, the government decided that it was impossible to defend the Channel Islands. On the 19th it was announced that

Above left: Children's Overseas Reception Board evacuees, called 'seavacuees', arriving in the USA, in 1940. (IWM HU 36219)

Above: Children's Overseas Reception Board letter dated October 1940, by which time overseas evacuation had been stopped owing to the sinking of ships by German U-boats.

all children were to be sent to the mainland the following day, with mothers accompanying those under school age. In all, 29,000 islanders were evacuated before the islands eventually fell on 1 July. Little in the way of luggage could be taken, usually just a single bag or suitcase. Islanders were taken by boat to Weymouth, and from there to various parts of Britain. Many were sent to Bury in Lancashire, others to Scotland, the West Country, Cheshire and the West Riding of Yorkshire; some even finished up in London!

The evacuees were virtually cut off from everyone they had left behind, who were now under enemy occupation. Every six to twelve months they might receive a Red Cross letter comprising twenty-five typed words. It was only natural, then, that the Channel Islanders in Britain formed a close-knit community; a committee was set up in London, and local Channel Isles societies sprang up, holding social get-togethers, Christmas parties and concerts.

Between July 1940 and July 1941, 12,000 evacuees from Gibraltar, many of them children, arrived in Britain. Many were billeted in hostels and hotels in London. Few spoke much English, and most of the children were taught in their hostels rather than integrated into local schools. In July 1944, with the advent of the V1 attacks on London, many were transferred to a purpose-built camp in Downpatrick in Northern Ireland.

A group of evacuees from the Channel Islands. By the time they returned in 1945, the older girls at the back would be young women.
(IWM D 738)

LATER EVACUATIONS

Had the German invasion taken place, there were plans for the complete evacuation of the coastal areas of East and West Sussex, Kent, and the south-east coast as far as Southend, involving three-quarters of a million people. This would take five days, using 1,000 trains and over 500 buses. The plan remained in place until November 1942, as invasion threats grew and then receded.

With the start of the Blitz on London in September 1940, steps were taken to re-evacuate the city, but once again the response was poor; during September only 20,500 unaccompanied children left home.

By late summer 1943, intelligence had been received of the threat of 'rocket bombs'; 100,000 were evacuated from the target areas in what was called Operation *Rivulet*. The V-weapons began to fall in June 1944, and evacuation began in earnest on 3 July. By mid-June 170,000 official evacuees had gone, plus about half a million private evacuees, rising to a total of almost 1.5 million by mid August, but almost immediately the figures began to fall again as a return started.

A Sunday club for evacuees and their visiting families being helped by local Girl Guides. Such clubs were a boon for billeters who often did not have the room to accommodate the large groups of relatives who might turn up.

END OF THE WAR

THE BRITISH GOVERNMENT announced the end of its official evacuation scheme on 7 September 1944. This, as it turned out, was rather premature; one day later the first V2 rocket fell on London, and a whole new wave of evacuees, both private and official, moved out of the city. Yet this did not last long; in spite of continued attack, by both V1 'doodlebugs' and V2s, within a few weeks the drift out of the cities soon dwindled and stopped, to be replaced by a flood of returning evacuees. Soon, the evacuation areas were, one by one, redesignated 'go home' areas, indicating that it was safe to return to them. By the start of 1945 only Hull and London had not yet been declared 'safe' - indeed this would not happen until 2 May, just six days before VE day.

The long-awaited homecoming often fell short of expectations. Many evacuees found their return as difficult as their leaving had been, having acquired new accents, new friends and new ways of life. For those who had left in 1939, many had spent half their young lives away from home, and the return home was no less of a wrench than their original departure. Family relationships had to be re-forged, not always an easy task; indeed some parents refused point-blank to have their children back, while some children refused to go back, and others, as a result of the bombing, had neither family nor home to go back to. Some had reached the age of fourteen, school-leaving age, while away and had started jobs, while some had acquired local sweethearts.

But on the whole most settled back in with a little effort all round, especially from fathers who had to come to grips with the fact that the small children who had left had now returned as young adults, most of whom had been forced by circumstances to become self-sufficient, and found attempts to reassert parental discipline extremely hard to take.

For some the reunion was even more traumatic, such as the 'seavacuees' who had spent five years in America; five years in which their only contact with home and family had been by letter. Photographs of them show well-fed teenagers with crew-cuts and bobby-sox, who now sailed back to austerity Britain, with its bomb sites and stringent food, clothing and sweet

Left: A welcome home card. In 1945 cards such as this were used both for returning troops and evacuees.

Below: 1945, and these rather self-assured looking young people are returning to Britain after five years of evacuation in Australia. (IWM HU 36233)

rationing. Others in a similar position were those evacuated from Gibraltar, while those from the German-occupied Channel Islands had had even less contact with their families, just two short Red Cross letters a year; for them the return was to barely remembered parents and homes.

Was evacuation a success? In a competition in the *Civil Defender*, an ARP newspaper, readers were asked to comment on various facets of the war. Two responses to the subject of evacuation were 'A fine scheme – for someone else's children' and 'A wonderful idea for those with a large family'. Evacuation certainly saved many lives, but far too often at a huge cost in terms of disrupted family life and education; for some the scars would take years to heal.

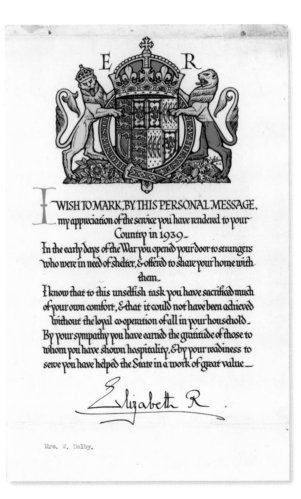

Certificate awarded in 1946 to all those who had taken in evacuees. The signature is that of Queen Elizabeth, wife of George VI, and future Queen Mother.

FURTHER READING

BOOKS

Bearing, Norah. *A Friendly Hearth*. Cape, 1946.

The British People at War. Odhams Press, *c*. 1944.

Carrick, Edward, and Bradley, Gerry. *Meet the Common People*. Studio, 1943.

Christian, Catherine. *The Big Test*. Girl Guides Association, 1947.

Deedes, William F. *ARP*. The *Daily Telegraph*, 1939.

Edelman, Maurice. *Production for Victory, Not Profit!* LBC, 1941.

Gloag, John. *Modern Publicity in War*. Studio, 1941.

Langdon Davies, John. *Air Raid*. Routledge, 1938.

Levien, J. W. J. *Atlas at War*. The Atlas Insurance Company, 1946.

Longmate, Norman. *How We Lived Then*. Hutchinson, 1971.

Moss, A. W. & Kirby, E. *Animals Were There*. Hutchinson, 1947.

Sillince, W. A. *We're All in it*. Collins, 1941.

Tisa, John (ed.). *The Palette and the Flame: Posters of the Spanish Civil War*. Collet's, 1980.

Titmuss, R. M. *Problems of Social Policy*. HMSO, 1950.

Worsley, Francis. *ITMA 1939–48*. Vox Mundi, 1948.

LEAFLETS AND BOOKLETS

Evacuation – why and how? HMSO, 1939.

The Householder's Handbook. HMSO, 1937.

The Schools in Wartime. HMSO, 1941.

War Emergency Instructions and Information. HMSO, 1939.

CONTEMPORARY PERIODICALS

Civil Defender

Daily Mirror

Daily Telegraph

Scouter

Sunday Dispatch

INDEX